Dedicated to
dreamers of all ages...

Inspired by PlayPumps International and
their work in Spontania, Mozambique.

Written by Matthew Eisenberg and Suneet Bhatt
Designed by Trupti Patel, Hina Sheth, and Amy Schmidt

ISBN: 1-4392-3810-3

At Dream Village, we use picture books and a website to help children explore and address important global issues.

Saved by the Well is a true story. The names of some characters have been changed to protect their privacy. We've also added a few characters to help the story along. But the places, events, and experiences discussed in the book are very real.

Jonzi (pronounced Jones + ee) and Jiji (pronounced Jee + Jee) are your Dream Village guides. They'll lead you through the book and our website.

Below are some important names and words you'll want to know before you start reading. Say them out loud and practice!

    Samora = Suh + more + uh

    Mozambique = Moe + zam + beek

    Spontania = Spon + tay + nee + ahh

Now let's get started!

Hi, I'm Jonzi! And I'm Jiji. We want to tell you a story about a good friend of ours, Samora.

Our friend Samora

Samora is 8-years old.
Like us, he likes to hang out, play
with friends, and go to school.

Samora lives in Mozambique,
a country in Africa. Africa is
far, far away—all the way on
the other side of the world!

Samora's family lives in a small, remote village. The name of the village is Spontania.

People in Spontania have to work hard for many things we take for granted—like food, education...

...and
clean
water.

When Spontania was built,
the settlers dug a well
that provided clean water
for everyone in the village.

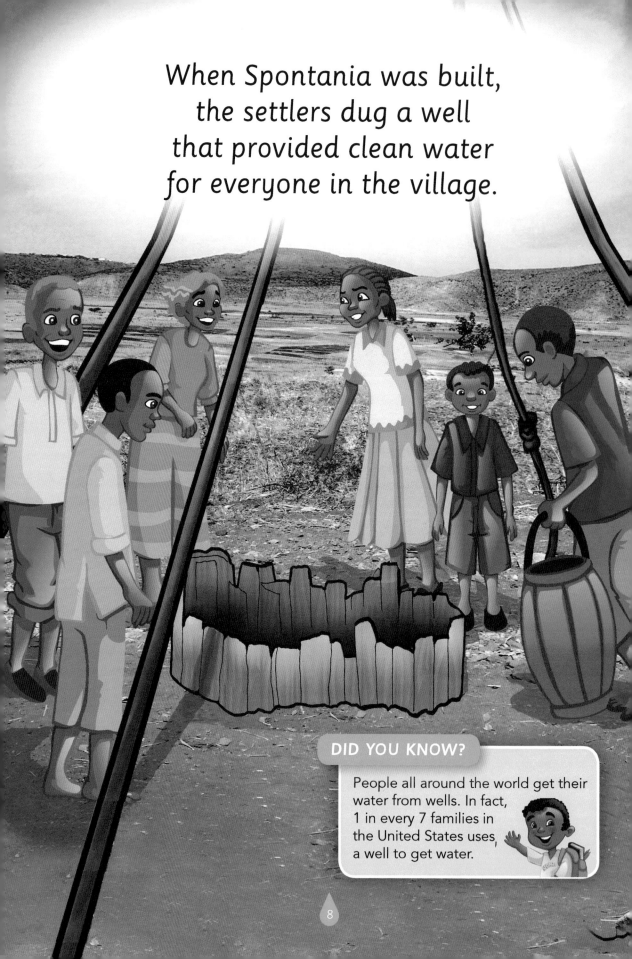

DID YOU KNOW?

People all around the world get their
water from wells. In fact,
1 in every 7 families in
the United States uses
a well to get water.

But Spontania kept growing.
Children were born.
New families arrived.
Soon, Spontania was
three times its original size!

The original well could not support
so many people, and it soon went dry.

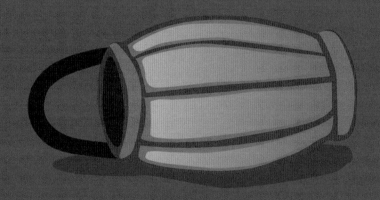

The well had been Spontania's only
source of clean water. Without it,
the village was in big trouble—where
would people get their water?

The closest source of clean water was a river. Unfortunately the river was many miles away, and the journey was dangerous.

Every day, Samora's mom
walked to the river and back
to get water for the family.

The journey was hard and took many hours.
Luckily, she was healthy and strong.

No one in Jose's family was strong enough to get water from the river. Instead, they had to drink water that was nearer to Spontania— water that was dirty and unsafe.

The
water
Jose's
family
drank
looked
like

MUD

THINK ABOUT IT

Compare this to the water you drink and use every day.

Drinking dirty water makes people sick.
Sick kids can't go to school.
Sick adults can't go to work.

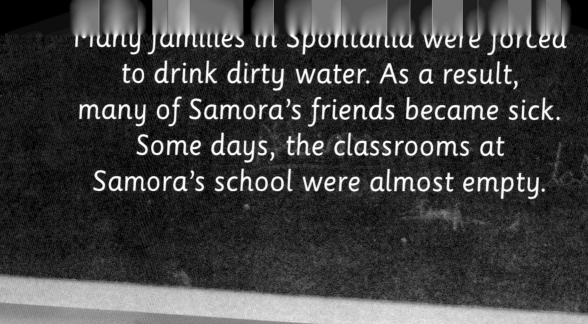

Many families in Spontania were forced
to drink dirty water. As a result,
many of Samora's friends became sick.
Some days, the classrooms at
Samora's school were almost empty.

Children were missing school,
which meant they weren't learning.
That wasn't good for their future,
or for the future of Spontania.

Spontania needed help.
Something had to change.

Luckily for Samora and his friends, something did change. Spontania got a brand new water pump that provided clean water for all the people in the village!

And it wasn't like any other pump they had ever seen. The new pump was special. It wasn't just a water pump...

...it was a
merry-go-round too!

When kids played on the merry-go-round, water was pumped into a big tank. That's why they called it the PlayPump water system—when kids played, water pumped!

③ Water is stored...

① Kids play...

② Water is pumped...

Water is shared!

④

DID YOU KNOW?

Water pumps create pressure that forces water deep in the ground to rise to the surface. The PlayPumps water tank can hold 660 gallons of water!

The PlayPump was installed in the yard behind Samora's school. Before the PlayPump, people had made a long and dangerous journey to get clean water. Now it was as simple as playing on a merry-go-round!

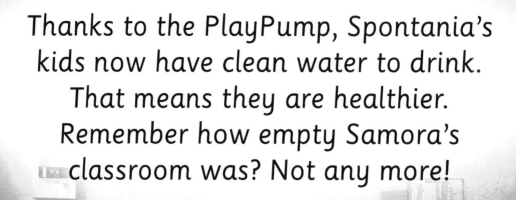

Thanks to the PlayPump, Spontania's kids now have clean water to drink. That means they are healthier. Remember how empty Samora's classroom was? Not any more!

DID YOU KNOW?

School teaches children important skills like reading, writing, and math. An education helps children have a better life when they grow up.

Girls can read and play too!

The PlayPump was especially exciting for the girls. Before, they spent their days getting water instead of going to school. That didn't seem fair. Now the girls have time to read and play, just like the boys!

The pump has helped the adults too. They use the water to grow fruits and vegetables. Samora's mom says that working in the garden is much easier than going to the river every day!

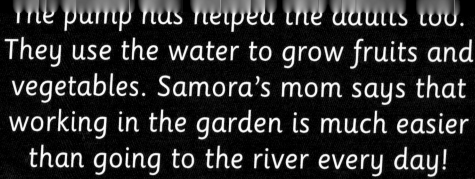

DID YOU KNOW?

Many people around the world go to bed hungry. The United Nations estimates that 1 in every 8 people don't have the food they need to survive.

The merry-go-round was the first
playground toy at Samora's school.
In fact, it's the only toy in the area.

As a result, Samora's school has become
a meeting place. Kids play on the PlayPump
while adults gather to talk to each other.

Helping neighbors!

The PlayPump solved Spontania's water problem. But other villages have water problems, too. That's why Spontania shares its pump and water with its neighbors.

Clean water has made life better for everyone in Spontania. Kids are going to school. Adults are working. Everyone is healthier, including Samora. That makes us happy, because he's our friend.

Samora is happy because he knows that he is helping Spontania when he plays.

"Even though I'm only 8-years old, I'm making the world around me a better place," he said. "It feels great to help other people."

DID YOU KNOW?

Samora and Jose are not the only kids who can help people. You can too! We'll teach you how at the end of this book.

Big smiles for everyone!

Spontania could not afford to buy a new pump for itself. PlayPumps International, a nonprofit organization, gave Spontania a new PlayPump water system...for free!

How did Spontania get the pump for free?

PlayPump donated by the Rotary clubs of:
Potters Bar
Brookmans Park   St Albans Priory
Berkhamsted Bullbourne Stevenage
            Hatfield   Harpenden Village
                        Rosebank

Donations make a difference

People who want to help others in need give money to organizations like PlayPumps International. PlayPumps International then uses that money to give pumps to villages like Spontania.

Organizations like PlayPumps International help people all around the world.

DID YOU KNOW?

PlayPumps International is just one of the many organizations that help provide clean water for people in need.

Without these organizations, Samora and the people of Spontania would still be struggling for clean water every single day.

Now, instead of worrying about water...

...Samora and his friends worry about who will get on the PlayPump first!

Building a Better Tomorrow - You can Help!

We introduced you to Samora so you could learn about some of the problems facing people in other parts of the world.

One of Spontania's biggest challenges was getting clean water. But that is not the only challenge that exists. Millions of people around the world face tough challenges every day. These challenges include finding enough food to eat and getting an education.

You can help people like Samora and the people of Spontania by visiting Dream Village and voting for a cause.

All you have to do is:

1

Visit Dream Village:
www.dream-village.org

2

Learn how you can help children
in Spontania and around the world

3

Vote for a cause by entering your
Dream Village Ticket Number and make
someone else's dream come true!

Your Dream Village Ticket Number is:

SBTW AMZN 7941 0905

Acknowledgements

Photo Credits

A majority of the photos in this book were provided to Dream Village directly by PlayPumps International. In some instances, Dream Village reached out to third parties for additional photography that we felt would enrich the story:

• Page 25: "Alive & Kicking Kenya," courtesy of Anne Holmstrom
• Page 8: Courtesy of Ronald Kato
• Pages 10, 11, & 22: Courtesy of CHF International (www.chfinternational.org/)

Illustration Credits

A variety of illustrators were involved in the creation of this book. Extra special thanks to:

• Trupti Patel, Co-designer, Director of Design and Illustration
  www.facebook.com/pages/Trupti-Art-Design/8871479140
• Hina Sheth, Co-designer, Director of Photography
  www.hinashethphotography.com
• Luisa Gonzaga, Creator of Jonzi and Jiji, Cover and Character Illustrations
  www.hahnsel.deviantart.com
• Richa Kinra, Background Illustration, Photo Integration
  www.coroflot.com/pinkdamselblack
• l3fty, who helped name Jonzi and Jiji
  www.coroflot.com/neontetramedia

Beta Tester Credits

This book would not have been possible without the feedback provided by beta testers from around the country. Their responses, often made based upon consultation with their children (students, sons, daughters, nieces, and nephews) were invaluable. Dream Village owes each of the following persons a tremendous debt of gratitude:

Meghan Breinig, Neha Rana, Jyoti Parekh, Anika Kamerkar, Amy Jones, Namrata Kakkar (and Walter, Jonah, Jacob, Milo, Hailey, Lily, Julia, Gaby, Megumi, Mona), Michelle Kelly, Sarah Leibowits de Luna, Julianna Trementozzi, Raki Desai, Julie Dulay, Raj Kanani, Bethany Frey, Meeta Gatonde, Lauren Gardner, Brett Alessi, Debbie Weiss, Shashank Sheth, Sue Moon, Pallavi Dixit, Melissa Corbett, Eileen Ryan, Laura Saenger, Stephanie Miller, Milloni Shah, Xavier Thomas, Sonali Kamerkar, Priya Chadha, and Jolie Chaikin.

An extra special thanks to Pinki Shah's 5th grade class at the Manhattan Country School (who also served as our video recommenders in the semi-final round with Echoing Green): Noah, Sophie, Kyle, Stefan, Kai, Mikah, Helena, Bradley, Altana, Ellie, Jamie, Margot, Maya, Khalil, Michael, Emma, Cara, Conor, Oni, Rebecca, and Isaiah.